Paying Attention:
A Guide to Wine with Food

Thank-you!

By Anthony Garcia

Edited by Chris Garcia

Published by Wine Is Divine
www.wineisdivine.com

Wine Is Divine
Austin, Texas

Edited by Chris Garcia

Printed in the United States of America

www.wineisdivine.com
info@wineisdivine.com

International Standard Book Number 0-9745458-0-5

To Chris Lanier (MLK)

Table of Contents

Preface
Page 7

Chapter 1- The Basics and The Theory Behind Selecting The
Right Wine with Food
Page 9

Chapter 2- Wine with Beef and Lamb
Page 19

Chapter 3- Wine with Chicken, Pork and Charcuterie
Page 29

Aged Riesling and Firne: An Essay
Page 37

Chapter 4- Wine with Seafood
Page 41

A Critic's Dilemma: An Essay
Page 49

Chapter 5- Wine with Desserts
Page 51

Hemingway, Wine & Detachment: An Essay
Page 56

Chapter 6- Pinot Noir
Page 59

Chapter 7- Garlic, Drinking What You Like and Paying
Attention
Page 67

"*You Don't Need a Guide, You Need a Glass*":
Two essays in one, how to learn about wine and an interview
with Greg Steiner of Grape Vine Market, Austin Texas
Page 69

Preface

This is the second time I've written this preface. Originally, I explained America's increased interest in wine and talked about the world's modern approach in making wine and many other things that you could find by picking up a book or surfing the web. Since you are reading this, you already know wine rules and, probably, you already have drawn your own conclusions on why you like it. More than likely, you really don't care why, or how, wine became a global phenomenon.

Instead, this preface will tell you how I approached writing this book and what you should expect from it.

I wrote this book trying to think like a chef; I learned about pairing wine with food by trying to think like a chef. I've paid attention to the culinary items I've sampled throughout the years and the wines I've enjoyed with them. I've learned through trial and error just like a chef. Chefs, in general, pay attention better than most professions of the world. If you over-salt a dish, it's gore. If you forget about what's in the oven, it's burnt. If you put the wrong type of herbs in the jus, it sucks. If you conceptualize the wrong sauce for the New Zealand lamb that you just paid a vast amount of dollars for, you blow it.

I've also learned from hanging with culinary professionals that simplicity rules. In a day when overwrought dishes show off a chef's creativity and consequently his greenness, it's the experienced cook that keeps the approach to food simple.

I owned a restaurant, Tocai, for a while and worked with some really great cooks. I taste wine constantly while always thinking about which foods it will pair with best. Put it simply: I paid attention to what I was doing.

Because of my love and respect for the chefs and cooks, I never want to devalue their efforts by selecting wines for my guests that don't suit their cuisine. A sommelier must select wines that suit the cuisine of his chef. This is his first priority.

I had no formal training before I wrote this book. In fact, I waited until the book was nearly finished before taking the first steps to obtain a Master Sommelier (MS) certification; this should take years I'm told. I wanted this book to have very little influence from other sources. I resisted reading *Wine Spectator* or any book on the topic of pairing wine with food. I wanted this, my first book, to be a *personal expression* of what I've learned. This was important to me.

Most of the research for this book came from my close working relationships with culinary professionals and their ability to tolerate and answer my plethora of crazy questions over the years. Then I tasted wine; I tasted their food, and I paid attention to both.

This book is broken down as follows: the first chapter covers the way I evaluate wine and the theory I've developed for pairing food with it. Then the following chapters cover every type of food an American can find here, in the States, and the wines that go with them. I also include a chapter on Pinot Noir.

I hope you enjoy and, more importantly, use this material.

Anthony Garcia

1

The Basics and The Theory Behind Selecting the Right Wine with Food

You Are In Charge

Wine is a very subjective thing. That is why the topic has writers and critics. If wine were an objective thing, we wouldn't need these people. When was the last time you've read a review on something constant like Coca-Cola? In wine, many things are not up for debate: What is the alcohol content and acidity? How was the wine vinified? What grapes are in the final blend? What is the vintage of the wine? Did the wine spend time in oak, or not? These questions are not subjective. Many elements, however, are up for evaluation. Does the wine have nuances of red fruits, citrus fruits, or orchard fruits? Are there nuances of fresh herbs or dried herbs? Is the wine full-bodied or medium-bodied? Remember this: one man's full-bodied wine is another man's medium-bodied wine.

One taster might say a wine has nuances of smoke and fresh herbs; another taster might say the same wine has nuances of roasted herbs. Both tasters probably sense the same thing but express it differently, while another taster might say the same wine has a fresh tarragon flavor. The cool thing about wine being subjective is that *the taster is empowered*, meaning it's up to you to decide what a wine tastes like not some guy who writes for a wine publication. I often disagree with wine reviews I read. My hope is that after you read this book, you will trust your own palate and not what some critic says.

Moreover, rely heavily upon your memories. If you think a wine smells like your grandmother's fresh baked scones with butter and red currants, then that's what you say. Who am I to disagree? I have often described certain wines as having confectionary notes, not meaning especially chocolate or vanilla but something more ethereal. When I recently returned to my hometown of Plymouth, Michigan, I was blown away when I walked into my childhood candy store. The smell was intoxicating, chocolates, hard candies, nuts, and confectionary paper. When I describe wine as having confectionary notes, I am really describing this store.

Getting to have the palate of a critic takes some time and practice, but the first thing you must do is begin thinking in terms of the wine's flavor nuances, in other words, how the wine reminds you of other things.

Before we get to the way I taste a wine, I want to cover two concepts:

A Wine Tasting as Something Smells

If I say a wine tastes like roses or has nuances of roses such as a Gewürztraminer. You might question, "Does this guy go around eating roses?" When a wine writer or I say a wine tastes like flowers what we are really saying is that the wine tastes as flowers smell. If a wine tastes like tobacco and cedar or has an essence of a cigar box such as with Chateauneuf-du-Pape, obviously I'm not eating or chewing on cedar and tobacco. What I am saying is this: *the wine tastes as a box of cigars smells.* This is a little tough to understand. When I'm describing a wine to guests and I use certain terms like cigar box or matchbook or chalk, I often receive perplexed looks, that is, until they taste the wine I'm recommending. Then they understand.

New World versus Old World

I'm going to use these terms often. So I'll take this opportunity to explain what they mean. Old World wines are the wines of Europe: France, Germany, Italy, Austria and others. New World wines are the wines of Australia, New Zealand, Latin America and the U.S. Old World wines tend to have high acidity. They are often earthy or mineral-like and their fruit is not as ripe as their New World counterparts. New World wines have riper fruit and lower acidity and higher alcohol. I am generalizing of course, but I need to clarify myself somehow.

How I Taste Wines

The wine's fruit itself can taste like other fruits. The first thing I smell and taste for is the other fruit nuances in the glass. Here are some examples of what a wine can smell and taste like:

Orchard Fruits- some wines contain nuances of apples, pears, and peaches. You will normally find that these fruit nuances are found in white wines.

Citrus Fruits- wines may contain nuances of grapefruit, oranges, tangerine, lime, and lemon, especially white wines from cooler climates such as the Loire Valley of France. The wines that have these nuances are mainly white although I definitely find citrus notes in red Burgundy, too.

Red Fruits- red wines mainly take on flavors of raspberries, cherries and strawberries such as Pinot Noir from Europe and the New World, Sangiovese from Chianti, Italy, and Grenache from the Rhone Valley of France. Some Rieslings from Germany have fresh cherry flavors.

Black Fruits- the popular Cabernet Sauvignon and Syrah or Shiraz often have flavors of blackberries, blueberries, and dark fruits.

Melons- Italian whites and Rieslings from the Old and New World often have flavors of cantaloupe and honeydew.

Tropical- you will find that if the growing region is warmer such as in Australia and California, then those whites will have flavors of mangos, pineapples, and papaya.

Dried Fruits- wines that hail from extremely warm climates such as Apulia—the heel of Italy—take on flavors of dried cherries or dates. Dessert wines that have been harvested late also take on flavors of dried fruits or ultra-ripe fruits.

<u>Cooked Fruit</u>- when a wine has the sweeter flavors of jams or compotes, they probably hail from warmer climates such as the New World. Does jam have as much acidity as fresh fruit? No. This term also implies a lower acidity found in the wine and a velvety mouth-feel.

I then focus my attention to the wine's earthy, herbaceous, spice qualities and wood nuances.

<u>Earthy Qualities</u>- some wines can smell like fresh mushrooms or musty damp earth and even like Old MacDonald's Farm such as Amarone from Veneto, Italy.

<u>Herbaceous Nuances</u>- wines can have nuances of fresh tarragon, basil, sage, oregano and so on. Some wines will smell like dried herbs such as what you would find in your cupboard. Some wines will have floral smells such as roses or gardenias. Other wines will have nuances of tobacco. Herbaceous qualities can be found in whites and reds of the New and Old World.

<u>Spices</u>- many wines have stronger spice nuances such as black and white pepper. Wines can also have flavors of baking spices such as clove, cinnamon and star of anise. Various spice nuances are found in wines from everyplace on the globe.

<u>Minerals</u>- wines that have mineral characteristics—such as flint or chalk—taste that way due to the soil where the wine is grown. Mineral-laden wines mainly hail from the Old World.

Smoke- some wines have notes of your backyard grill and others have the "I just walked in to a barbecue joint" flavor. You will find that Nebbiolo-based wines from Piedmont, Italy carry smoke flavors among other grapes such as aged Rieslings from Germany.

Confectionary Notes- wines can smell and taste like vanilla or chocolate or other sugar spun items. The sweeter, riper wines of the New World carry these flavors often.

Wood- wood flavors in wine come from the oak that the wine was aged in. The two most common woods are American Oak and French Oak. American Oak is the least subtle; it will impart flavors of intense vanilla, coconut, dill, and board. French Oak is more delicate; it will impart flavors of subtle vanilla, nutmeg, and cream. In some cases, wines—such as with Grenache based wines from the Southern Rhone Valley in France—smell and taste like cedar even though the wine was not aged in any wood.

Texture and Weight

The next thing I look for is the texture and weight. What does the wine feel like in your mouth? Is it dense, full-bodied? Is the wine light or medium-bodied? Is it silky, velvety or syrupy having viscosity? Is it austere, meaning having a high degree of acid without enough fruit to balance it out?

Tannins and Acidity

The next things I taste for are tannins and acidity. Tannins are a natural byproduct of fermentation. Tannins are found in the seeds, stems and skins of grapes. White wines usually do not have tannins because the juice is removed from the skins immediately. Red wines spend time with their skins and, thus, gain color and tannic structure. Tannins are antioxidants that will break down over time. This is why red wines age better than white wines. Have you ever tasted tannins? Yes. When you bite into a fresh grape, you have probably noticed that the sweet juice is underneath the chalky dry skin. That dry chalky stuff is where the tannins are found.

Acid is a little easier to recognize. All fruits have acid. Some fruits have a lot of acid such as citrus. Others, like watermelon, have less acid. When you make wine, the natural acid from the grapes goes into the wine. White wines that are considered dry have a lot of acid in them. White wines that have tons of acid and big fruit flavors will age for years such as the 1959 Rieslings from Germany which can age for 100 years. The acid that is in wine is very important in pairing the wine with food. We will get to that later.

The last thing I taste for is the wine's finish or how long after the wine is swallowed do you still taste it—*the longer the better.*

Through all of this, you should be able to notice if the wine is sweet, dry, or somewhere in between.

The Basic Theory for Pairing Wine with Food

A) Balance or match the weight of the wine with the weight of the dish. Never let the weight of dish supersede the body of the wine and vice versa. You would not want to pair a heavy red, such as a powerful Zinfandel, with a delicate piece of fish. You would not want to pair a juicy steak with a light white wine.

B) Make sure the wine has acid. If it doesn't, then do not attempt to pair it with food unless the dish has an acidic or vinaigrette component to it. I will elaborate on this concept later in the chapters that follow.

C) Always pair the subtleties of the dish and the wine together. This is what I call a *bridge,* the shared nuances of the wine and the dish. I use the word subtleties because at the same time you are trying to find the *bridge,* you also don't want to exaggerate the similarities such as pairing a rich, buttery dish of risotto with a rich, buttery and low acid American Chardonnay or pairing an acidic, citrus-like Sauvignon Blanc from Sancerre in the Loire Valley of France with a citrus vinaigrette salad. Do not over-accentuate the shared flavors.

You do want to pair roasted lamb with a Cote Rotie—a Syrah from France—having notes of game. For me subtleties are like being in love. When you are in love, there are obvious elements that draw you to your partner—maybe, he or she is a good or honest person or perhaps you share similar interests or values. That's the big picture, but it is my opinion that it is the subtle things that your partner does that are poignant. In great cuisine, a chef might use the best ingredients from around the world, but it is his or her subtleties in the preparation that make a dish succeed.

D) Lastly, know the dish and know the wine. If you were looking for some short cuts, this book will not offer any. You still will need to know what the wine tastes like before pairing it with food. This means knowing the wine for yourself or trusting the wine steward (dining out) or wine retailer (cooking at home) before you purchase it. After this book, hopefully, you will have enough ammunition to ask the appropriate questions.

Now if what I just wrote clicks, then stop reading and go out and experiment. If you feel like you need more information, then the following chapters will give you examples of wine paired with food.

This is a barrel being made at Chateau Margaux. On site, they make 37% of their barrels.

2

Wine with Beef and Lamb

Beef and lamb are the easiest meats to pair with wine. These heavier meats require heavier, full-bodied wines. You will probably be sticking mainly to red wine, but some whites will work well, too. For white wine lovers, just make sure weight of the wine matches the weight of the meat.

The wine's acidity will play an important roll based on the meat's cooking preparation. I will cover the major ways meats are prepared; then I will suggest the wines I've found to be my favorites with these different types of fare. I'll group lamb and beef together for the purpose of an easy explanation, and I'll include a small section on burgers and what makes lamb what it is.

Grilled Meats

Grilling meats implies fire cooking the meat. You usually have a charcoal element or a wood element creating the fire. Charcoal grilling imparts a carbon and more burnt flavor. When I say burnt, I don't mean ruined; I mean parts of the meat will have slightly roasted, slightly bitter flavors. This is a good thing. Have you ever had a roasted or grilled tomato marinara or a roasted tomato salsa or hot sauce where you can see and taste little tiny pieces of burnt tomato skin? It's kind of like that.

What goes with meats prepared in this manner? The best wines are sweeter and richer reds that have riper fruit and an element of oak. Why? Sweet ripe fruit goes with grilled notes that are slightly bitter. Oak, whether it's American or French, will impart notes of vanilla that sweeten up the slightly carbon flavor of the meats.

If you've ever visited a high dollar steak house, you'll notice that rich, full-bodied California Cabernet Sauvignon dominates their wine list. These wines are full-bodied and are oaked heavily. It's not just the weight of the wine matching the weight of the meat, it's also the sweetness of these wines that pair so well with grilled meats.

Heavier Old World wines such as Bordeaux from France and Brunello from Italy also work great. I especially prefer juicy Old World wines that hail from warm, ripe vintages.

If the grilling method is by way of wood, then you have other wine options to consider. Wood grilled meats will still have a *burnt* quality, but they will also have a smoked flavor. If I prefer wines with sweeter notes for charcoal grilling because of the inherent contrast, then for wood grilling, I prefer wines that have a *bridge* or a shared nuance. Syrahs from the Northern Rhone Valley—because of their smoky quality—are my favorite wines for wood grilled meats. I want to caution again, do not overdo it; try to be subtle. Pinotage, a variety from South Africa, has extremely smoky nuances that I think over-accentuates wood grilled meats. You don't ever want to have too much smoke flavor across your palate unless you just, absolutely, love it.

Seared Meats

Seared meats rule. The meat's outside is rapidly cooked to seal in the juicy flesh underneath. Normally, after a piece of meat is seared, it is then further cooked or heated—perhaps in an oven—until the meat is finished or the fat has rendered throughout the entire piece. Since seared meats are inherently succulent, you should pair them with wines of higher acidity. The acid will act as a *foil* to the juicy, succulent flavors. I love Italian reds with higher acidity for seared meats, Barbera from Piedmont or Brunello from Tuscany. You don't have to stay in Italy, but make sure that your wine has medium to high acidity.

Smoked Meats or Texas-Style Barbecue

I graduated from high school and college in Texas, and I haven't really left the state since. In Texas, barbecue is a religion. What goes on barbecue? Tasty, juicy sauce. Why? Smoked meats, especially Texas-style barbecue, can sometimes be rather dry. Or put another way, barbecue isn't exactly like a rare steak. A zesty barbecue sauce, of course, imparts acid and flavor to the meat, but it also makes the dish less dry. It gives the dish what it needs most, moisture. I am not saying make the wine taste like barbecue sauce, but make the wine like the *essence* of the sauce. The wine should be juicy such as with New World reds.

Sometimes it's good to think of the wine as an alcoholic sauce. Then think of the traditional accompaniment for the dish. Make the wine similar to the *essence* of the traditional accompaniment.

Braised and Roasted Meats

These preparations refer to slow oven-cooked methods for lamb and beef. Braising is slightly browning or searing the meat, then cooking it *covered* at a low to moderate heat. Roasting is similar but the method is *uncovered.* I am not going to explain these methods in great detail. I am going to tell you what the final product tastes like—when cooked properly—and which wines go with this type of fare.

Slow cooked meats will be ultra succulent and sometimes gelatinous such as with short ribs, oxtail, ossobuco—made of young lamb or calf—and mom's, good old-fashioned, pot roast. Everything in the dish is moist and succulent: the meat, the braising or roasting jus and the vegetables that accompanied the meat as it was cooking.

What do these food items need? Acidity. You must have a contrast to the richness and moisture of the dish. If the dish is ultra-gelatinous such as with braised short ribs or ossobuco, then you are going to definitely need wines of high acid to cut through that texture. Old World wines are the perfect match because of their medium to high acid levels and their inherent earthy flavors or rustic flavors that give you the perfect *bridge.*

Avoid wines of the New World for slow cooked items. Heavy ripe fruit with high alcohol, low acidity and high viscosity will combine with the meat's richness to overpower your palate. The wine must have moderate to high acidity for slow roasted meats.

Raw Meat

My experience with raw meats is really based upon several *amuse bouche*—a small beginning appetizer—prepared by my friend, Chef Chris Lanier, whom I've had the pleasure to work with. He would often create a steak tartare mixing capers and herbs in finely diced beef atop a handmade cracker with a touch of vinaigrette. My favorite wine to pair with his steak tartare was Sauvignon Blanc from the Loire Valley of France. The tartare is juicy and tender. Chris would use the vinaigrette as a contrast to the juiciness. Sauvignon Blanc from the Loire such as Cheverny, Sancerre, and Pouilly-Fume was the perfect compliment. These wines are extremely acidic and have nuances of citrus and caraway seed. You don't have to select the whites of the Loire, but you do have to select high acid wines with raw meat.

Meats and Their Sauces

Sauces for meats vary from the rich demi-glace or bordelaise sauce—based on broth or stock—to the niçoise relish of vinegar, diced tomatoes, olives, olive oil, onions, capers and artichokes. I'll make this simple. If the sauce is acidic, pair a low acid wine with it—New World. If the sauce is rich, pair a moderate to highly acidic wine with it—Old World.

The Burger

I wanted to include something about an American food item we are all very familiar with and my thoughts on an American wine with this item. I have cautioned you not to over-accentuate the similarities between the wine and the dish, what I called the *bridge*. In certain instances, if the dish is in no way subtle, then the wine shouldn't be either. In the fine dining tradition, there is a time-honored wine/food match up, the mighty Foie Gras and the majestic Sauternes.

Foie Gras is a rich unctuous goose liver that when seared becomes one of the most decadent dishes in the world. It is normally served with a bread or brioche element and sweet accompanying sauces. The traditional wine counterpart to the dish is Bordeaux's Sauternes, a late harvest dessert wine of Semillon and Sauvignon Blanc, which becomes infected with a beneficial mold called *Botrytis Cinerea* or *Noble Rot.*

Both products are complex, meaning they carry several flavor nuances. Both products have unique textures. They are not the subtlest of species or, to put it another way, they are as subtle as royalty is allowed to be. Let me add that the pairing does work. The thick, unctuous liquid with the delicate fatty, almost slimy, liver balances well. The "botrytis funk," as I call it, a honeyed stinkiness, goes very well with the inherent multi-flavors in the goose liver. The wine's sweetness and acidity accentuates the dish well.

But does this exception hold true for only two of the most venerated food and wine items in the world? No. I think the *Foie Gras/Sauternes model* applies to the burger and the Zinfandel. I like burgers with cheese, bacon, lettuce, sliced tomatoes, and mayo. Think of the burger's several flavors and textures: toasted bread (the bun), mayonnaise, tomato slices, lettuce, bacon, cheese, meat, and the bread again underneath.

Now think of how you eat this product, bite by bite: taking in a small part of each ingredient at the same time. To me, it's a rather decadent experience and, oh, so American. Now give me a Zinfandel that doesn't hold back: full-bodied, viscous, oaky, spicy, moderate acidity and mucho alcohol: Big, Dense and Intense.

The weight of the wine will balance with the weight of the meat, and the acid will cut through all the multi-textures and flavors, livening them up. The oak and spice lend themselves very well to the bacon and mayo and any grilled notes. The wine's viscosity acts as a slightly sweet blanket combining the flavors together, and the high alcohol gives the experience an overall sense of power.

The big Zinfandel and burger should always walk the fine line between harmony and chaos.

26

Lamb and Its Inherent Flavor

One time at my old restaurant, Tocai, a customer asked if the lamb we served was "lamby." We thought that was pretty funny, like saying is the beef *beefy*. After I thought about it awhile, I was ashamed of myself because some lamb is pretty damn *lamby* while other lamb is quite mild like beef. It is this essence, call it *lamby*, call it *gamey*, call it *strong-flavored*, which makes lamb what it is, and certain wines just plain rule with this product.

My first choices for lamb are the wines of the Rhone Valley, both north and south. France's Rhone Valley has two distinct micro climates the hot southern part, home to Cotes-du-Rhone, Chateaunuef-du-Pape, Gigondas, and Vacqueyras, to name a few, and the predominantly cooler northern part home to Cote Rotie, St. Joseph, Hermitage, and Cornas. The red wines of the north are made of Syrah, and these wines carry a wonderful *gamey* characteristic among other qualities such as the aforementioned smoky nuance. These are my favorites with lamb.

The wines of the south are blends primarily of Grenache then Syrah, but the vintner can use up to thirteen varietals in the final blend. While these wines are less *gamey* than their Northern Rhone counterparts, they still have excellent notes of game to them, and because of their Grenache component, they carry a wonderful *cedar* quality (like a cigar box). This cedar quality, also, goes very well with lamb.

In addition to France's Rhone Valley, I also love Sangiovese and Brunello based wines from Central Italy. These wines tend to have *leather* notes to them, and along with *cedar*, *leather* and lamb also create something even more elevated when combined. These French and Italian wines also have wonderful earth and herb nuances.

At this point, I don't want to cause any controversy from the Bordeaux and Burgundy camps or any aficionados of other wine regions for that matter. Many wines go well with lamb, but I find something a little more essential about the wines of the Rhone Valley and Central Italy.

This is a diverse selection of wines that pair with chicken & pork: New World Chardonnay, Vouvray, Pinot Grigio, Southern French, Cotes-du-Rhone & Rioja.

3

Wine with Chicken, Pork and Charcuterie

I get excited when I think of the myriad of wine options when pairing with chicken, pork, and charcuterie. I grouped theses food items together because both red wine and white wine work well. Let me define charcuterie for those that find the term new. Charcuterie are those deli-type items: pâté, terrines, rillettes, cold cuts, sausages—meat items that have a higher fat content to them. In this chapter, I will be discussing pork and chicken together; then I will have a section on other types of bird, and I conclude with charcuterie.

Chicken and Pork with Wine

I hope not to offend anyone by discussing chicken and pork together. It is the best way to organize this chapter, and it is no coincidence pork is hailed as "the other white meat." They share similarities, and chicken and pork work well with the same types of wine for just about the same reasons.

Chicken and Pork and Their Weight

Chicken and pork are not dense meats. They are lighter than beef and lamb but heavier than fish and seafood. What does this mean? Practically speaking, it means you can pair white wine and red wine with pork and chicken. The weight of the wine must be in harmony with the weight of the dish. Whites with weight and light to medium-bodied reds will work well.

Chicken, Pork and Their Preparation

A theme of this chapter is versatility. Pork and chicken are prepared in many different ways: grilled, roasted or baked or rotisserie, pan-fried, and deep-fried. Let's not forget these meats are also marinated or even breaded more often than their four legged cousins beef and lamb. Some preparations are lean—George Forman Grill style—while others, again I'm showing my Texas roots, are fatty or greasy such as a nice greasy pork chop with mashed potatoes and candied carrots. All of these differences allow you to have more fun in pairing with wine.

Fat Content, Acidity and Breading

First thing, you will want to ask yourself if the dish is lean or fatty? When I say fatty, I mean hot and viscous not cold and solid, as in charcuterie. Why? For fatty or greasy dishes, whether you choose a red or a white wine, it is best to select acidic, grease cutting, palate brightening wines. For leaner dishes, you'll want to pair juicier, richness adding wines.

Second thing, will your dish be acidic or have a vinegar presence? Remember, creamier, oaky wines compliment acidic dishes. If your dish is starchy (chicken and rice), then acid adding wines are the way to go.

Third thing, will you be breading and frying your meat? Again, selecting a wine with acid is best. Acid will cut through the beading and the oil.

To summarize, pair New World wines with leaner and more acidic dishes, and pair Old World wines with breaded and fattier dishes.

Roasted Items

For roasted items such as rotisserie chicken—slow roasted, herb crusted, skin on, fat in, juicy, and succulent or oven-roasted pork chops with garlic cloves, tomatoes and new potatoes, rustic and tasty—it is time to unload the drier reds and whites. Again, acid is needed to cut through the skin or fat. For other rustic meals—such as my favorite chicken dish, *Coq au Vin*, a red wine marinated and braised chicken dish with bacon, carrots, shallots, onions, mushrooms and potatoes—I like rustic wines. I recently compared a Cotes-du-Rhone, a red Burgundy, and an Oregon Pinot Noir as a pairing for this dish. All were great, but I liked the Cotes-du-Rhone the best.

Grilled Items

For grilled products, I like wines that have richness and sweetness to them. Riesling and Chenin Blanc from the Loire Valley of France give the smoky, grilled, carbon-flavor on the meat the sweetness it deserves. I didn't make this up. Think about barbecued chicken. You buy a bottle; then you put it on the meat, and you grill it. Why? Grilled and sweet work together. Remember what I said in Chapter 2; sometimes it's good to think of the wine as an alcoholic sauce. Richer Chardonnay with tropical nuances and other fat white wine will work well, too.

Red wines also work great with grilled products. Make sure the reds you choose are juicy. They should be forward with fruit. I enjoy Rioja and other Tempranillo-based wines from Spain because of their weight, their fruit-forwardness, and their use of oak that lends itself to grilled flavors. I do not like drier, tannic wines with grilled pork or chicken; the drying sensation of these wines accentuates the grilled notes in an astringent manner.

The Difference Between Pairing a Red and Pairing a White

A cook may find that when creating a dish that is roasted, herbaceous and peppery, it is easier to find a red that suits it. This is true. Reds take on more savory flavor nuances than whites do. So finding a red wine that suits the dish is much easier. Let's say you purchased a tropical or citrusy white wine; then maybe have Hawaiian Chicken or make an orange glaze for the dish. Have the fruit nuances of the dish mingle with the fruit nuances of the wine.

Maybe you are planning on roasting chicken, mashing potatoes, and steaming some vegetables, plain and simple. Maybe the addition of the wine is all you need. That's my point. Chicken and pork are inexpensive ways to eat. Go out and pick yourself up an inexpensive wine; elevate the simple dinner. You'll be happy and so will your retailer.

Other Types of Bird

I didn't go into every type of bird here. What I will say is to use the same principles explained above in your pairings. I will add this: if the bird is drier, such as pheasant, pair a juicier wine with it. If the bird is oilier, such as duck, pair a drier wine with it. Some birds are quite gamey. Depending on your palate, pair wines that will accentuate this, such as Southern Rhone reds, or downplay this with a California Pinot Noir.

Charcuterie and Wine

Above, I gave a very general description for charcuterie. Those examples I listed can be made from chicken, duck, goose, lamb, pork, beef, and even seafood products. They sublimely vary in texture and flavor. What they hold in common is a higher fat content, and that fat content is cold and solid, contrasting with the hot and viscous fat I discussed earlier in this chapter.

If fat that is hot and unctuous needs an acidic wine, is fat that is cold and solid also in need of acidity? Yes, but there is also a big difference. Charcuterie needs a similarity of texture, a *textural bridge*.

The wines that work best with charcuterie are unctuous. A hot and greasy dish does not work well with oily, viscous wines; the similarity is excessively off-putting. In the case of charcuterie, wines with oily richness, sweeter flavor, and underlying acidity give the charcuterie what it needs: a similarity of texture completely inter-twined with a contrast of acidity.

Thus, the best wines for charcuterie are Riesling and Chenin Blanc. Other whites such as Sauternes and Gewürztraminer also work great. Reds like Pinot Noir are also great due to their silky texture, sweet red fruit nuances, and renowned acidity. I also like rustic reds with coarse-textured charcuterie such as country-style pâté or pork rillette paired with inexpensive reds of the Languedoc-Roussillon region of France.

During a trip to Germany, I sampled many old Rieslings: '53, '59, '63, '75, '76, '81 & '83. This was one of my favorites. The price on old Rieslings in the Mosel is ridiculously inexpensive. This bottle cost me $18.

In the Rheingau, at Weil, this winemaker, Jochen Becker-Köhn, taught me a great deal bout Riesling.

Aged Riesling and Firne: An Essay written on
November 7th, 2002 after a tasting at Robert Weil,
Rheingau, Germany

I probably should wait to write about my European trip
after I return to the states—you know put a little
distance between the continent and myself—to collect
my thoughts. Screw it! I just left Weingut Robert Weil
and have to put down what happened. I've learned
something that I've been searching for a long while.

When I pulled up to the Weil estate, I realized that I
didn't charge my camera battery. I knew that I would
have to ask winemaker Jochen Becker-Köhn if I could
charge my battery—I had another appointment with
Wegeler later that day, and I would need to have my
camera working. I'm sort of bashful about asking for
certain things so, needless to say, I was already a little
anxious before even entering one of Germany's most
famous estates.

The thing I didn't expect about Germany was this
hardcore, sincere hospitality. Germans are super
friendly. What ya'll need to know is that I purposefully
came over while the Rheingau, Rheinhessen, and Mosel
are still harvesting. Guys like me are really the last
people winemakers want to see during their busiest
time, but that's what I wanted to see, the harvest, that
weird anxious time when everything is thoroughly at
the will of Mother Nature, and the air at wineries
during the harvest is way different. You smell yeast
and fruit and earth; it's strange. You literally smell the
estate long after you've left it. That smell stays in your
nostrils. I'm not kidding.

Jochen Becker-Köhn was extremely kind to me. He toured me around the facilities. I got to see the Kiedrich Gräfenberg vineyard and their impressive cellar cataloging their Riesling dated back to the 1800's. Unfortunately, my battery went dead when I was in the cellar. The exchange of ideas was fun. He talked in length on the 2001 vintage, which was stellar, and the winemaking style of Weil across the board, a delicate purity that you can tell even in the color of each wine. I let him know about America's new facination with Riesling and my customers reaction to his 1999 Riesling Auslese, Kiedricher Gräfenberg that I sell by the glass and pair with Chef Chris Lanier's Hudson Valley Seared Foie Gras. I also gave him my views on American late harvest Riesling, which I won't share with you.

Then we began tasting through the 2001s (It was at this time I asked to charge my battery, my fault!):

2001 Rheingau Riesling Qualitätswein Trocken
2001 Kiedricher Gräfenberg Riesling Erstes Gewächs
     (1st Growth) Trocken
2001 Rhiengau Riesling Qualitätswein
2001 Rheingau Riesling Kabinett
2001 Kiedricher Gräfenberg Riesling Spätlese
2001 Kiedricher Gräfenberg Riesling Auslese
     Goldkapsel

All the wines were amazing. The tasting took a different course when I asked to re-taste the 2001 Kiedricher Gräfenberg Riesling Auslese Goldkapsel. It's very important to slow yourself down a little when tasting in this manner. You don't want to miss anything, and that's the reason why I'm over here to taste wine and learn. I wanted to make sure about an aspect of the wine before I gave my opinion, especially on this prestigious wine set for auction. After my re-taste, I think I said something like this, "What an amazing almond and honey quality this wine has." He agreed. Then we talked of the myriad of ways a Riesling could taste. Next he asked me to wait a moment as he left the room. He returned with a 1976 Kiedricher Gräfenberg Riesling Auslese, one of their best ever. I was honored and thought to myself *I must've done something right.*

Of course, the 1976 was one of the best things I have put in my mouth. There is nothing like an old Riesling. Then I explained to him the problem that I have with the word *petrol* and Riesling. *Petrol* is a common critic's term for the way an older Riesling smells. By the way *petrol* is a good thing. Anyway, I stated something like, "Yeah, it's a descriptor that does apply sometimes . . . I think the term might be overused . . . It's a word that probably frightens newer wine devotees . . . and there is this other taste that is in old Rieslings that's not quite petrol, and I feel that using petrol might be wrong." He explained that what I'm talking about is *Firne* (FEAR-nah), the smell of aging. His grandfather used to always talk about it. There is a point that goes beyond petrol. It's brilliant that the Germans have a word for it.

At this juncture, I sort of freaked out, as I do when I learn something huge. I explained that I've been looking for this word for a long time. I then described the dilemma I have with my old Bordeaux. I have guests whom ask me about my older selections in the cellar, but I have to always ask if it's their first experience with an older wine. We as Americans grow up on young wine, and if it is the first time you've ever had an aged wine you might think, "Wow, this sucks," such as when I tried beer at the age of five. So when, in fact, they say, "Yes, this is the first time," I then explain what an aged wine is all about. I always take the first taste, and then after they sample it I say, "You know that thing you can't put your finger on, that crazy ethereal essence: that's aging." The Germans say *Firne*.

I'm delighted because now I have another way of describing old wines to neophytes. In my business you want to get the customer what he wants, and you also want to educate the guest on other wines. When the wines are sometimes $700 and up, the more you educate the better.

After the tasting, I was blissfully on my way. I'm sure I will think of this day for a long while. Several things happened. I was blown away by the sincere hospitality. I saw the beautiful estate and cellar. I was able to give a little knowledge about the U.S. I learned about *Firne*. I tried amazing wines, and I was even impressed with myself for asking to charge my battery, which is something that is a little difficult for me—I know, I'm a freak.

Thank-you Jochen Becker-Köhn and Weingut Robert Weil.

4

Wine with Seafood

I have some reservations about including this seafood chapter. I think it might look arrogant on my part to give my opinions on such a vast topic, but I have been blessed in working with many kinds of seafood. Thankfully, my work conditions are far away from the *salmon/tuna model* common to many restaurants in the U.S. I still have to add this disclaimer. Do I know more about *Loup de Mer* than a native of the Provençal Coast? Do I understand *Dorade* better than a local that lives on the Île de Noirmoutier in the Bay of Biscay? Do I know more about *Arctic Char* than an Icelandic fisherman? The answer is no. It's no shocker that we started off this book with beef. As a nation, we are raised on beef, and the wines we produce in this county manifest this fact. Because of this reason, I have experimented with seafood more than the other meats of the world, and I found the answer of pairing wine with seafood to be simple.

Weight is Key

First and foremost, the weight of the wine is the most important factor. If you overpower a seafood dish with a heavy wine, you ruin the dish and the hard work it took to pull it out of the sea, prepare it, cook it, and serve it. Seafood products are less forgiving than their land counterparts when it comes to pairing wine with them.

Acid is Key

Seafood calls for acid more than the other meats. What comes with fried calamari, fish and chips, or paella? Lemon. The acid and seafood combination is fundamental. If you are already making an extremely acidic sauce, then the wine should be less acidic but still essential.

Texture is Key

Texture matching is the tougher part. It is quintessentially comparing the subtleties, a *textural bridge*. A wine's texture is something that is *tasted and felt*. Matching the texture of the wine to the texture of the seafood is important, but sometimes it is better to have the wine mimic the dish's traditional acidic accompaniments; I will discuss this below.

I organized this chapter by the types of seafood that I see as being common to us as Americans. Following this list, I give my theories and examples of the kinds of wines that pair with these fare:

A) Raw Seafood
B) Buttery Textured Seafood
C) Delicate Textured Seafood
D) "Steaky" Textured Seafood
E) Salmonoids
F) Cajun and Spicy Seafood
G) Fried Seafood
H) Crustaceans
I) Mollusks

Raw Seafood

Items such as raw or almost-raw tuna need a wine with more body and viscosity. I prefer red wine with raw tuna. A good New Zealand Pinot Noir that is soft, viscous and has higher acidity is sublime with tuna. Try Pinot from Oregon, too.

Items like raw oysters require a contrast more than a comparison of texture. Raw oysters are mucous-like; thus, having an unctuously textured wine is too much. Introduce a wine that is light and acidic analogous to the lemon served with most raw oysters. My favorite wine with raw oysters is non-vintage Brut Champagne, something refreshing and acidic. I do not like **aged** vintage Champagne with raw seafood because of their complex and often yeasty characteristics. Keep it simple and inexpensive; go with the non-vintage Champagne or select a Cava from Spain. Traditionally made Chablis as well as Muscadet from the Loire Valley compliment raw oysters brilliantly, also.

Buttery Textured Seafood

These items can range in weight from the more delicate Seabass to the thicker skate or denser scallops. The trick here is to introduce a wine that matches the weight, has acid and has a creamy texture. Whites that are barrel aged such as Meursault or more acidic versions of California Chardonnay, work great with buttery textured seafood.

Delicate Textured Seafood

If you are worried about a fish falling apart on you during the cooking process, then why overpower the dish with a heavy wine after it is served? Delicate textured seafood includes items such as Halibut, Turbot, and Flounder (your flatfish). I will reiterate fish is less forgiving than their land counterparts as far as weight is concerned. Go with light wines such as crisp European whites and light, less oaky New World whites. In Spain, they have these wines called *Vino de Aguja* (Needle Wine). They are dry, light, and slightly effervescent with citrus notes that go with Spain's seafood fare; unfortunately, I have never seen them stateside.

"Steaky" Textured Seafood

As the name indicates, "steaky" fish is reminiscent of steak— items that are thicker and sometimes drier than other kinds of seafood—such as shark, swordfish and monkfish. These products demand heavier wines. If these products are grilled, they require a juicier wine, something that contrasts the grilled notes and unfortunately the *sometimes* drier, overcooked qualities. Select rich white wines hailing from the New World. I also appreciate red Rioja with "steaky" textured seafood.

Salmonoids

These are items related to salmon and trout such as Artic Char, Truite de Mer (European Ocean Trout), Wild Salmon and Farmed-Raised Salmon. There is no greater combination with these fish than Pinot Noir. They have a distinctive flavor and a *weighty/ethereal* fatty quality. Pinot Noir—because of its weight, viscosity, acid, and sweetness of fruit—with Salmonoids is one of the most sublime combinations in cuisine. The sweetness of fruit goes with the natural distinctive flavor of the fish; the texture of the wine and the fattiness of the fish match, and the acidity cuts through the fish and the wine together.

Cajun and Spicy Seafood

Another great food wine combination is the sweet to off-dry Riesling or Chenin Blanc with spicy seafood. I remember one spring, my first mentor, Rob Forman, was leaving town. I threw a going away party/crawfish boil. The wine distributors all donated Riesling to the affair. Man, what a day! The sweetness of the wine and the spicy flavors contrast and thus compliment each other very well. The acid of the wine slightly accentuates without intensifying the dish. The spicy flavors and the viscosity of the wine act as a sort of organic blanket holding all the flavors together. Try this with spicy Thai food, too.

Fried Seafood

You know this category well. Chances are you grew up in a hamburger, hotdog, fish sticks household; restaurant chains are based on this product, and remember the Irish pub explosion of the 1990's? What accompanies fried fish or fish and chips? Lemon wedges, malt vinegar, and sharp cocktail sauce. They are the acidic accompaniments and the wines should be also, such as non-oaked Sauvignon Blanc and crisp Italian whites. They cut through that breading and wake up the mouth.

Crustaceans

Crab and the rarified lobster are two items that many people would like to eat everyday if they could. Matching the texture is very important. Think creamy. Think buttery: crab cakes pan-fried in butter, lobster with drawn butter. Have wines that are rich, unctuous, and creamy. Make sure the wines you choose also have a good dose of acidity or else the experience becomes insipid. I like creamier examples of Viognier—especially Condreiu—and full white Burgundy. New World expressions are good; be careful to select ones with acid.

Mollusks

I am speaking here of cooked mollusks, clams, oysters, and mussels. We have quite a few Italian restaurants in the U.S. One dish that you might find at an Italian café is steamed mussels or clams in white wine and extra virgin olive oil with capers and garlic and onions. Selecting light and acidic white wines is the ticket such as Pinot Grigio, Albariño, Soave, Gavi, inexpensive Sauvignon Blanc from France's Loire Valley and, let's not forget, Southern French Rosé. Again, we are looking for acidity to brighten up the dish, accentuating the flavors.

Pairing wine with seafood is not as difficult as it seems. Just pay attention to what you are eating or cooking. Sometimes you'll want the wine to mimic the dish's traditional counterparts—such as with fried seafood—and other times you'll want the wine to have more of a textural match, such as with Salmonoids. If you have spicy seafood, a sweet yet acidic wine provides the contrast needed. For the most part, acid is a welcome addition to any seafood dish.

These are wines you'll enjoy with seafood: New World Chardonnay for "steaky" seafood, Cava with oysters, Burgundy (Pinot Noir) with salmon, Meursault with lobster & crab, and Gavi with steamed mussels.

A Critic's Dilemma: **An Essay**

The greatest pitfall a critic of anything faces is relying heavily on what is familiar, or worse yet, panning what is unfamiliar. Critics are critics because they are a) analytical and b) experienced. Therein lies the pitfall. Once you get to a certain point of experience these two poles, analysis and experience, *may* play against each other.

Sometimes critics come across something new, new subjects, new media, new flavors, etc. These new "things" may baffle them because they have never encountered them before. The situation is worsened, especially, if the critics' experience has contributed to a false sense of security, or worse yet, an ego, which can lead to ignorance and even dismissal of what's new.

I, as a critic of wine, come across things that are foreign to me. I would blow it, if I actually panned new things. I would not do myself, or anyone else, any good if I dismissed those new things that were previously unknown by my *grand* experience.

This pitfall doesn't apply only to wine and food critics but to all critics. I recently purchased the 2002 DVD release of David Lynch's *Blue Velvet*. The DVD includes a 1986 review by Siskel and Ebert. Roger Ebert, arguably the most powerful movie critic in the U.S., gave it the "thumbs down." I won't go into a recap, but I will say he blew it. His experience got the best of his analytical brain. He had never witnessed actors being subjected to this type of material, and he got upset. I loved the movie.

When you are watching or reading a critic's critique, pay close attention; are they liking things they only recognize and dismissing the rest? If they are, they are blowing it by making the mistake that what they recognize is a sign of *their* good taste.

In Champagne, here is one of many riddling racks deep under the city of Reims in Taittinger's cellars dating back to the 4th century A.D. Their massive cellar was carved out of chalk which was a popular building material during Roman times.

5

Wine with Desserts

I originally didn't plan to include theory on pairing wine with desserts. This is a hotly debated topic, and I think that I really wanted to stay off the subject. I realized this would be a copout, as I do have something to say, and I have experimented continually throughout the years with dessert and dessert wines.

How You Drink a Dessert Wine Is Important

In the restaurant setting, I've noticed that by the dessert course the pace of the dinner slows down dramatically: stomachs are contented, conversations are less fluid, and breathing is deeper. In addition, desserts are more likely to be savored bite by bite. In fact, any good pastry chef wants you to know that everything on the plate is important. The sauces and accompaniments are as important as the featured pastry item. Not that a good savory chef thinks you should blow off his sauce, starch, and vegetable accompaniments and only pay attention to his meats, but let's be logical for a moment. There is an order or *ranking of preference* that most humans consider when thinking about savory food. It is as follows:

1) Meats
2) Starches
3) Vegetables

It's like this: "Let's go get some fried chicken . . . I went through the drive-thru because I was craving some fries . . . That place has the best bread." It is rarely like this: "Damn, I have a craving for some haricot vert . . . Let's go out and grab some swiss chard."

Desserts are taken as a whole. The ice cream is as important as the pie, if you will. Desserts are sweet and intense and are eaten for the most part very slowly; a diner will savor every bite (and sometimes roll their eyes in ecstasy). Dessert wines are sweet and intense. Why do you think the proper glassware is so small? And you should drink them slowly savoring every sip. In my work places, I've seen tables of guests quickly eat their savory courses and drink their accompanying wine, but when dessert is served, the guests slow down.

You do not slam down a glass of Tawny Port or Sauternes with your dessert. You savor the wine. I believe that it is appropriate to serve the dessert wine before the dessert is served and encourage the guest to sip on it and let the wine act as an alcoholic *amuse bouche* getting the mind and palate ready for the dessert course. When the dessert is served, the wine should be sipped carefully letting it act as an alcoholic sauce. Finally, save some dessert wine for after the dessert is finished. Let the wine act as an alcoholic chaser washing down all the sweet flavors.

What Wine You Drink with Dessert Is Important

The wine must be very sweet or else when the dessert is eaten it will overpower the wine making it taste flavorless. Normal still wines are not good with dessert. Dry, sparkling wines are good with light fruit sorbets because the acid in the wine and the acid in the sorbet combine to create harmony. For the most part, the wines must be sweet.

The Dessert Wine Should Be Inexpensive

You didn't think I'd throw this one at you, did you? Really rare Vintage Port or Trockenbeerenauslesen (TBAs) or aged Sauternes should stand alone. They require a tremendous effort and patience in their production and storage. You take away what they are when you attempt a food match. When I'm talking about pairing desserts with dessert wine, I'm talking about selecting inexpensive wines such as Moscato d'Asti, Tawny Ports, Late Harvest Wines, or Banyuls. They do exist!

Chocolate Desserts

I like fortified wines or *vin doux naturel* with chocolate desserts. Tawny Ports and younger Banyuls from France's Languedoc-Roussillon region are great with chocolate. A Tawny Port will impart a nutty, vanilla quality to the dessert. A young Banyuls offers a fruit compote aspect to desserts alongside its own chocolate and spice nuances. The Tawny Ports should also be younger, ten years or less; the reason is: as the wine goes up in years, it becomes lighter, more ethereal, which is not suitable for heavier chocolate desserts. You want some weight in your wine with chocolate unless it is a mousse. Then go lighter with the fortified wine.

Fruit Desserts

I like non-fortified late harvest or dried grape wines with fruit desserts such as Italy's Torcolato or France's Loupiac and Sauternes (only if it's an inexpensive one). These wines' fruit nuances mingle very well with these types of desserts, and if the dish has spices such as clove, nutmeg, ginger or cinnamon, these wines become absolutely poetic.

Nutty Desserts

You have much more versatility when your desserts are nutty. Ports work great. Late harvest wines are great. Banyuls rules as do other types of *vin doux naturel* such as Muscat de St-Jean de Minervois. They are all going to impart confectionary nuances to your dessert.

Pastry-Driven Desserts

If the dessert has a dominant breading element, such as bread pudding or pie, and especially if you have some vanilla ice cream accompanying it, I prefer the sweet and lightly effervescent Moscato d'Asti from Italy. Moscato d'Asti has a touch more noticeable acidity to contrast the breading, and it combines fruit and light vanilla nuances. They are wonderfully inexpensive, too.

Ice Creams

Just as with nutty desserts, with ice cream you have a vaster array of wine options. It will be useful to think of the dessert wine as an alcoholic sauce, like a topping.

The moral of the story is please enjoy dessert with dessert wines. It is often an overlooked pleasure. There are many reasonably priced dessert wines on the market. These inexpensive wines will enhance your meal without taking too much away from your pocketbook.

Hemingway, Wine & Detachment: An Essay

"I went in and ate dinner. It was a big meal for France but it seemed very carefully apportioned after Spain. I drank a bottle of wine for company. It was a Chateau Margaux. It was pleasant to be drinking slowly and to be tasting the wine and to be drinking alone. A bottle of wine was good company."

An excerpt from *The Sun Also Rises*

A long time ago I read an essay that Norman Mailer wrote in *Advertisements for Myself.* He stated that one should imagine that Hemingway's protagonist is Hemingway himself. The fact that Hemingway had a rich life, filled with adventure, made the stories so much more appealing. He added that if Hemingway was a squirrelly sort of chap, then the stories would be less appealing.

I state this now because when I read *The Sun Also Rises,* I find that I really don't picture a Jake Barnes character. I picture Earnest Hemingway, and I certainly don't picture Tyrone Power from the movie version. So from here on out, when I refer to something Jake Barnes experienced, I'm just going to say Hemingway.

So when Hemingway wrote in *The Sun Also Rises* that he drank a bottle of wine for company he wasn't kidding. In this, my favorite book, he starts off the book as a loner and ends the book as a loner (technically, he's riding in a car with Lady Brett Ashley in Madrid, but he is really alone). Between the beginning and the end of the book, he becomes more disillusioned with his friends and more disillusioned with humanity. He's hurt by the woman that he loves, and there's not much he can do about it, so he takes comfort in a good bottle of wine and a good meal. I love this part of the book because I've done it hundreds of times myself.

Being alone with a good bottle of wine is very comforting, and, in many ways, it is also like being on a first date.

Drinking wine brings to mind several questions: Where did you come from? What's the climate like there? What are you really like? How were you treated before now? Also, like a first date, the a wine needs a little time after the cork is pulled before it opens up to you. For me this ritual gives an immense amount of comfort.

Sharing a bottle with friends is also a great experience, but there is something more analytical about drinking wine alone. I believe that great wine tasters almost have to be loners. They should possess a certain detachment, like Hemingway, so that they can learn and then depict their experience to others.

This is Louis Jadot's hi-tech winemaking facility in Beaune. Don't let the size or the modernity fool you. Jadot produces terroir driven Burgundy.

6

Pinot Noir

I do not believe that this book could finish without a chapter dedicated to Pinot Noir. I do not want to go into the stories of its history, its prestige, or its difficulty in production. There is plenty of information for you to research in books, magazines, and on-line if you want to learn more—also other people would put it more eloquently and with more fervor than I could. I'll state this: Pinot Noir is a versatile varietal, meaning it can go with an array of foods. That rules.

Heavier Pinot Noirs can stand up to heavier meats such as beef, lamb, poultry, and pork. Lighter Pinot Noirs are perfect for seafood but more particularly Salmonoids—see Chapter 4.

The Profile of Pinot Noir

Depending on where it is from, Pinot Noir can exhibit many flavor nuances: dark and red fruits, cooked, dried and fresh fruits, dried and fresh herbs, sweet and strong herbs, spices, minerals, or even smoke, but it is Pinot Noir's texture and acidity that make it go well with food.

I decided to flip the script on you. I'm going to break down Pinot Noir by geographic area and give the foods I like with them instead of starting with food as I have done in previous chapters.

Burgundy- The Old World

I feel bad that I'm not going to talk about Pinot Nero from the cooler climates of Italy or Spätburgunder from Germany—especially the amazing *Hochheimer Riechestal* Spätburgunders from Künstler in the Rheingau—because my experience with colder climate Old World Pinot Noir is mainly Burgundy, which isn't a bad thing because Burgundy rules, and they are more readily available to you here in the U.S.A.

With Burgundy, I pretty much like everything: with lamb it's great; with duck and poultry it rules; beef works; with Salmonoids it is sublime; risotto dishes are some of my favorites when paired with Pinot, and with sautéed mushrooms—yikes! Just make sure the weight of the Pinot Noir and the weight of the dish match; the acidity and texture of wine will enhance the rest.

A Burgundian Boast

Historically speaking, Burgundians are known to be proud and self-aggrandizing. Let's not forget these are the people responsible for siding with the British and burning Jeanne D'Arc at the stake at a time when France was about to become England. Anyway, I was reading an account of a Burgundian response to Pinot Noir being grown in other places on the globe. The writer indicated Burgundy's supremacy for producing the world's best Pinot Noir, due to the fact that

Pinot Noir is the best grape to display Burgundian soil or *terroir.* Since the rest of the world doesn't have this soil—which it doesn't—then there is no way Burgundy could ever be topped.

This is a pretty indefeasible position, and it is probably true. Let me paraphrase: since Pinot Noir is the best delivery vehicle for the greatest soil on earth, and since this soil is only found in Burgundy, then we can conclude that Burgundy has the best Pinot Noir on the planet. Remember in Michael Mann's *The Insider* when Russell Crow kept referring to cigarettes as *delivery vehicles for nicotine?* It's kind of like that.

Why am I telling you all this? I believe that Pinot Noir lends itself best not just to the soil of Burgundy but also lends itself best to savory food (not including spicy, fiery cuisine, of course). That's just Pinot Noir's nature.

Pinot Noir of the New World

After reading the preceding account of Burgundies, you might be thinking to yourself, "Why should I continue with the rest of the world if Burgundy is so supreme?" I'll state this: there are excellent Pinot Noirs produced in the New World.

Drink New World Pinot Noir with Heavier Dishes

For the most part, because of our hotter climate, Pinot Noir here—and in other New World regions—is riper, richer, has higher alcohol, and is less acidic. There are foods that go great with this type of Pinot Noir. I love a steak with an ultra rich New World Pinot Noir. Once I conducted a Pinot Noir tasting and wine pairing class where the last flight was a Californian Central Coast Pinot Noir with a mini cheeseburger. Everyone's melon was twisted after that revelation. You can pair thicker Pinot Noir with other types of heavy dishes, but don't overpower lighter seafood with it.

Drink New World Pinot Noir with Acidic Dishes

More chefs and cooks use vinaigrettes to enhance their dishes nowadays. New World Pinot Noir is perfect for pairing cuisine with vinaigrettes due to its less acidic nature. I do not like acidic Old World Pinot Noir with acidic dishes, too much acid. I'll remind you: Make sure that the wine's weight or body doesn't overpower the dish, and you'll be fine.

An Example of Pinot Noir's Versatility

One night three guests proposed a challenge to me. They were going to order an array of items from our menu. They wanted me to pick a wine to go with all of the courses.

They ordered:

First Course:

Diver Scallops—wrapped in bacon—with a sautéed ceps, porcini mushrooms from France, parsnip puree, and a carrot Riesling jus.

Cassoulet—a French casserole—with duck confit, rice beans, breadcrumbs, parsley, and sausage.

Maine Steelhead Trout—potato wrapped and slow roasted—with winter greens and root vegetables, and a citrus vinaigrette.

Main Course:

Roasted New Zealand Venison with milk braised salsify, sweet potato, sautéed wintergreens, and venison jus.

Pot-au-Feu—the all in one pot brothy meal—with braised pork belly, short ribs and air chilled chicken with winter vegetables and savoy cabbage.

Monkfish—bacon wrapped and roasted—with artichoke barigoule, a stew of wild mushrooms, bacon, tomato, artichokes, and shaved black truffles.

The wine I selected was:

1998 Leroy Vosne-Romanee, *Les Beaux Monts,* **1er Cru, Cote de Nuits, Burgundy**

The wine was a ruby red color with a bouquet of sweet cooked and fresh red fruits, light citrus and vanilla notes, perfumy exotic spices and soft herbs, but mainly a tarragon flavor. The palate displayed all that the nose displayed but also had moderate acidity and low tannins with a medium-bodied constitution and an ultra silky mouth-feel.

The Diver Scallops Pairing- This was really the toughest pairing of the bunch, but it came out beautifully. The carrot Riesling jus and parsnip puree possessed sweet flavors that the Burgundy's moderate acidity contrasted well with. The texture of the wine and the texture of the scallops matched. The earthy mushrooms combined well with the sweet fruit flavors of the wine.

The Cassoulet Pairing- This was the easiest to pair with the wine, and Pinot and duck are traditional counterparts. The oily nature of the duck and sausage matched well with the silky texture of the Vosne-Romanee. The moderate acidity cut through all of the Cassoulet's textures: the beans, the breadcrumbs, and the meats. The fruit and herbaceous quality of the wine complimented the dish wonderfully.

The Steelhead Pairing- This was sublime. The slow-roasted, well-rendered fat of the salmonoid and the silky, unctuous texture of the wine was a perfect match. The acid of the wine contrasted well with all of the textures of the dish. Our chef,

Chris Lanier's, citrus vinaigrette was not too acidic, and the wine's acid was moderate, so they matched well together, but it was the light citrus notes of the wine with the citrus vinaigrette that I thought was to die for.

The Venison Pairing- I feared the wine might have been a touch light before I selected it, but this was not so; they complimented each other to the tee. Remember with meats you have more leeway than with seafood concerning the weight. The jus and the herbal elements of the wine combined superbly. My favorite part of the dish was the vanilla notes of the wine complimenting the sweet potato— which was first put into a hot dry pan for a quick-sear and then put into a slow simmer of chicken broth, displaying sweet and savory flavors—and the milk-braised salsify. Then the acidity of the wine cut through these two worthy starches beautifully.

The Pot-au-Feu Pairing- This was a winner. The wine's weight was well suited to all the meats and broth. The acid of the wine was a great addition to the dish, which could use a little acid for sure. A French dish with a French wine.

The Monkfish Pairing- This was a no brainer. The bacon and the sweet fruit flavors ruled together. The acid was needed to perk up the barigoule. The truffles with the wine's vanilla and perfumy exotic spices *just make ya wanna holla*. The weight of the wine was a match to the heavier Monkfish.

I want to add that the wine in my example was an expensive one, but these cats could afford the two bottles they sucked down. Less expensive Burgundy would have worked well, too.

There you have it. Pinot Noir is versatile and supreme when combined with varied cuisine. I sincerely wish you already love Pinot Noir. If for some reason you do not like Pinot Noir—I understand that they may seem light compared to the American bent for thicker Cabernet Sauvignon—please keep trying them. I promise you that time will come when everything clicks.

7

Garlic, Drinking What You Like and Paying Attention

I'm wrapping up this book, and I want to say a few things about garlic, drinking what you like, and paying attention.

Garlic

I think there is a misconception about garlic and wine. I've heard people group garlic with excessive cologne wearing as a destroyer of wine. Now cologne is a "no-no" at a wine tasting because you don't want to interfere with your palate and sense of smell or anyone else's for that matter. While consuming garlic won't interfere with someone else's palate—unless you are kissing them—garlic will interfere with your palate because **garlic makes wine taste great, period.** It is just such an incredibly strong flavored food item that lingers for a long time. It is for this reason that I love inexpensive—and mainly Italian—wine with garlic-oriented dishes.

Garlic interacts with the wine's fruit acidity creating this wonderful dance on your tongue. I like nice inexpensive Italian whites with garlicky steamed mussels or with Middle Eastern favorites such as baba ghanoush and hummus. I like inexpensive reds with garlicky pasta and bread dishes. If you are spending more money on a complex wine, then you should avoid garlic because it will overpower the wine, and you won't truly be able to evaluate the wine, but with cheap wine garlic rules.

Drinking What You Like

No matter how much I explain *this goes with that and that goes with this,* you should always drink what gives you pleasure. You only like red wine, fine. Whites are your thing, cool. Can you still apply these theories to find the perfect white wine for a steak? Sure you can. One's taste is his or her own; it should never be heckled or debated, such as making fun of someone who likes his steak cooked well-done. One should not judge.

Just Pay Attention

The way I learned about pairing wine with food is by simply paying close attention. As with most things in the world, if you pay attention to what's going on, you'll have an easier time at work, in your personal life, or in pursuing your hobbies. Concentrate on the items you are eating: What's going to be on the plate? How is it prepared? After you know what is on the plate, then you can select the right wine.

If the wine selection happened before the meal, let's say you purchased a wine recommended by your trusted retailer: How did he say the wine would taste? Is it full-bodied? Is it acidic? Is it herbaceous? Pay attention to these indications, and you'll prepare the right meal. All you have to do is experiment a little on your own, and you'll get the hang of it, and the payoff is juicy. You give yourself a tremendous amount of pleasure when you select the right wine with the right dish or prepare the right dish with the selected wine.

"You Don't Need a Guide, You Need a Glass": Two essays in one, how to learn about wine and an interview with Greg Steiner of Grape Vine Market, Austin, Texas

The title of the article is a quote from my friend, Steven Harding. The statement is true. Books and magazines are good tools to use when learning wine, but ultimately it is what's in the glass that gives you the real pleasure and knowledge. Let's say you are just now getting into wine and you are at the next level where America must be left behind in order to see what the rest of the world's wines are like. Can you learn about this subject without spending too much money? Yes.

If you are a beginner at anything, be it golf or mountain bike riding or photography, you don't start off by buying the most expensive equipment. You start off with a modest and inexpensive set of clubs or bike or camera. First, you might find out you hate your new hobby then, "Oops, now I own a $3000.00 bike, My Fault!" or "Honey, do you think I'll be able to get some of my money back by selling this Hasselblad camera on ebay?" Second, you may not ever become so advanced that you'll ever need the most expensive equipment. You start off modest, and if you get the hang of it, or when you start to advance, then buy the next echelon up. Why should learning about and enjoying wine be any different?

For wine, if you are going to learn about it, you do not go out and buy the most expensive bottles from around the world. Economically, it doesn't make sense and this could turn you off about the whole process all together, so don't do it.

Go to a wine store with a reputation for integrity. Bring about 100 or so bucks, and say, "I want a mixed case of wine from all over the world." Tell the guy you want to spend an average of no more than $10.00 per bottle, and you want 12 different bottles, and just for kicks ban American wine. Here's the cool thing: most stores offer a case discount of 10 or 15 percent even on mixed cases, so you'll fall under $120.00 for the visit.

Drink the wine over a couple three weeks and see what you like; see if it leads you to want to learn about how that wine was put in the bottle in the first place. Or maybe you'll want to learn more about Spanish wines or Italian and so on. I recommend doing this with a friend. Split the cost and compare notes with each other.

I called up my friend Greg Steiner of Grape Vine Market on a hot Tuesday afternoon and said, "Hey, man I'm writing an article on how to inexpensively learn about wine. I'm coming in to buy a mixed case, and treat me as if I am a novice." He agreed. I showed up with my digital voice recorder, and we toured his 18,000 square foot store with a shopping cart. The experience was amazing. The following is a recount of the isle-by-isle tour as recorded digitally:

We head to the front of the store where Greg pulls a bottle from a case stack. It is **2001 Theo Minges, Riesling, Halbtroken, Pfalz- $11.49**. And check it out; it's a full liter!

<u>Greg</u>: "Just because it's made of Riesling doesn't make it sweet. It's a halbtroken, so it's half dry. It's got some fruit to it but it's light and it's crisp. When we buy wines, we are always thinking what are we going to pair this with . . .Why are we

buying this? Sometimes, we buy things that are expensive because we know people want it; other times, we buy wines because a certain food type item goes with it, but we're in Texas . . .It's hot. When we buy these things [the wine], we think: sitting on the patio, sitting at the pool, going to the lake, going down to Zilker Park and watching the musical in the park. You want something you can drink that's cool."

Me: "Would you call this a crossover wine, if somebody wanted to get into Germany, would you call this not so shockingly sweet?"

Greg: "Yeah, you could take this that way (as he places the wine in the cart). So many people think of German wines as sweet, but they're not."

Next we head over to Grape Vine's Italian section and Greg picks up a new favorite of mine, the 2000 Castelvero Barbera, Piemonte- $7.99.

Me: (playing the novice) "Now I've seen Barbera from Asti and Alba, what is this Piemonte thing (as I point to the word on the label)?"

Greg: "Alba and Asti are both cities in the area of Piedmont which is in the northwest corner of Italy, and if you come over here and look at this map we have over here (we stroll over to one of Grape Vine's large hanging maps, this one of Italy), you see that northwestern corner of Italy, that's Piedmont. It's surrounded on three sides by the Alps, like a horseshoe that faces out toward the rest of Italy. This [the Barbera] doesn't come from either Asti or Alba. It comes from outside those zones designated for those cities, so it's not as expensive, but it's great."

Me: "What would you pair this wine with?"

Greg: "I would pair it with pizza."

Now Greg stays in Italy, and he hands me the **1999 Colosi, Sicilia- $8.99.**

Me: "Now this looks like a Sicilian wine."

Greg: "This is where the Godfather's from. The whole big shooting spree went on down there." (I interrupt)

Me: "Would this be considered a Dago Red?" (He cracks up, laughing) "O.K. Good- now other producers are producing great wine in this area like the Planeta people who else?"

Greg: "The Regaleali folks."

Now Greg takes me to his tasting counter and offers me something which just came in from Spain the **2000 Tresantos, Zamora, Spain- $9.99**

Greg: "This has been opened and registered with the TABC three days ago." (That's the law, baby).

Me: "Who imports this?"

Greg: "It's from an importer called Jorge Ordoñez."

<u>Me</u>: "I heard he might be a super guy, is that true?"

<u>Greg</u>: "He brings the best Spanish portfolio into America. . . and we registered tasting this with the TABC three days ago."

<u>Me</u>: "Excellent. So we are totally in compliance."

<u>Greg</u>: "We couldn't be any more compliant."

<u>Me</u>: "So, we should give a big *shout out* to the TABC, holding it down, letting me kick it at Grape Vine." (Greg starts to laugh again) "I like it. I'll take a bottle. Would you call this wine soft?"

<u>Greg</u>: "Yes, but it also has a vibrancy to it, and it's deep. It has some dark qualities to it . . .dark cherry, black cherry."

Greg then suggested Alsace, France that was Germany between 1870 through 1919. He gives me a bottle of **2000 Pierre Sparr, Pinot Blanc Reserve- $9.99.**

<u>Me</u>: "I notice that this [wine] tells me what I'm getting. Is that odd for France?"

<u>Greg</u>: "Alsace is simple. Every time you look at a bottle of Alsatian wine the biggest thing is the name (the producer of the wine). Then when you see the grape varietal on the label, every single ounce of that wine is that grape variety . . .this is crisp and light and floral and perfumed and wonderful."

Now Greg takes me to the flipside of the Alsace isle to the white Bordeaux section. He gives me the **2000 Chateau Grand-Jean, Entre-Deux-Mer, Bordeaux- $7.99**

<u>Me</u>: "Entre-Deux-Mer, between the two seas, right?"

<u>Greg</u>: "You know why it says that? It's between the rivers Dordogne and Garonne and where those two rivers come together to form the Gironde [river]. Everything between those two rivers is basically white wine. That's your Entre-Deux-Mer area. Everything to the north is going to be your red wine. Everything to the left of that river [Garonne meeting Gironde] is going to be cab-based [Cabernet Sauvignon] wines, and everything to the right [of the Dordogne], or *right bank,* is going to be Merlot based."

<u>Me</u>: "Is this Entre-Deux-Mer more Sauvignon Blanc or more Semillon?"

<u>Greg</u>: "It's probably 55% - 45%, Sauvignon Blanc over Semillon."

We go to Portugal next for Green Wine or Vinho Verde. The **2001 Arca Nova, Vinho Verde- $6.99**, a light refreshing *sneak it into Barton Springs Pool Wine.*

At this point <u>**Greg**</u> adds: "I tell people all the time, 'You've got something in here (pointing to the shopping cart) where every single one of these wines are completely different from each other, and these will all be flavors that won't be foreign to you, like something weird and wacky, but just different. On your receipt, everything is listed out, so keep your receipt. Then later come back and find me again and tell me what you liked . . .I have to get to know what you like. This is why this store has over 5000 labels. Why do we have them? Because we want to get you what you like. You go home and try these wines in settings we talked about, sitting out by the pool, maybe with a little food. You do that and you see what you think.'"

Now we go to Australia, where Greg recommends one red and one white: **2001 Rosemont Estate Grencahe/Shiraz- $6.99** and the **2001 Yellow Tail, Chardonnay- $6.99.** Both of these wines hail from South Eastern Australia.

<u>Me</u>: "Now I know the Rosemont, but the Yellow Tail I'm not familiar with, great label"

<u>Greg</u>: "It's kind of like California where you get all that tropical fruit, and it's shockingly good."

Greg then suggests the **2001 Charles Back,** *Goats do Roam,* **South Africa- $8.79.**

<u>Me</u>: "Hey, *Goats do Roam,* like maybe a take on the Cotes-du-Rhone and another great label. I'm noticing great labels here on the inexpensive stuff."

Greg's next selection is a white Burgundy the **2000 Coron Pere et Fils, Bourgogne Blanc- $12.99** because you have to have a white Burgundy (Chardonnay) in the mix.

At this point, I see that I'm going to come way under my budget, especially with Grape Vine's 15% case discount. So, I decide to add an inexpensive Australian Port to the order, and Greg gives me the **non-vintage Clock Tower Australian Tawny Port- $10.49**, and then we make it thirteen selections with the 2000 George Dubœuf, *Domaine Desmures,* Chiroubles, Beaujolais- $8.29

<u>Greg</u>: "Let's stay in Burgundy and finish out with reds. 2000 was one of the great years for Beaujolais. They are not expensive. They're easy drinking. They go with every kind of food. Whenever you hear the term red Burgundy, you are talking Pinot Noir. When you hear the term white Burgundy, you are talking Chardonnay, but when you get down to the south, the southern tip of Burgundy, there's an area called Beaujolais, and some people think it shouldn't be part of Burgundy, but it is and the grape there is Gamay."

<u>Greg</u> (then goes over all the wine again, summarizing the selections he made, then he adds): "When you're done, you go home, and you try them and come back and tell me what you thought. I expect you to like all these things [the wine] but I don't think you will because your palate is not exactly my palate. Tell me what you like, but most importantly tell me what you don't like, because I learn more about somebody's palate by what they didn't like as compared to what they liked."

We stroll to the front check out, and I am happily surprised when all thirteen bottles cost a mere $100.27. I encourage everyone who wants to learn about wine to try this method. I had a blast hanging with Greg Steiner and, as you can tell by his own words he knows a bunch about the subject of wine. He has the enthusiasm and charisma to pass along this information in a totally non-snobby manner.

Thanks to Greg Steiner and Grape Vine Market.

Grape Vine Market, Austin, Texas

In Vouvray, that's me with Philippe Foreau, one of my favorite winemakers. The Loire Valley rules.

Coming Soon

Never Save Your Fork:
An Insider's Guide to Restaurant Service

&

for more writings by Anthony Garcia
check-out
www.wineisdivine.com